T0129097

AN INTUITIONISTIC WAY TO ULTIMATE REALITY

Unlocking the Mysteries of Man and His Universe

FARAZ GODREJ JOSHI

Archway Publishing books may be ordered through booksellers or by contacting:

Archway Publishing
1663 Liberty Drive
Bloomington, IN 47403
www.archwaypublishing.com
1 (888) 242-5904

Because of the dynamic nature of the Internet, any web addresses or links contained in this book may have changed since publication and may no longer be valid. The views expressed in this work are solely those of the author and do not necessarily reflect the views of the publisher, and the publisher hereby disclaims any responsibility for them.

Any people depicted in stock imagery provided by Getty Images are models, and such images are being used for illustrative purposes only. Certain stock imagery © Getty Images.

ISBN: 978-1-4808-7141-0 (sc)
ISBN: 978-1-4808-7142-7 (hc)
ISBN: 978-1-4808-7140-3 (e)

Library of Congress Control Number: 2018913321

Print information available on the last page.

Archway Publishing rev. date: 05/22/2019

To my beloved
Parents and siblings,
Wife and children

A thousand crusaders stopped and froze,
And into their minds a new doubt arose;
Then, a dawning revelation concerning 'why',
Pale and lonely in a vast sky.

How May One Approach This Book?

There may not be any one unique approach but the power of the intuitionistic method is a recurring theme. Theories based on these themes can be judged on how well they affirm basic intuitions and yield acceptable results. An assortment of some of the most celebrated metaphysical and metamathematical problems are intuitionistically resolved.

In particular, 'cyclicity' or 'eternal recurrence' is proved and this immediately puts Determinism on a firm footing since if time is cyclic, the universe is obviously deterministic. Indeed, without cyclicity, the very concept of Determinism ceases to have meaning since no distinguishing criterion for it then exists.

Other than cyclicity, which applies to the universe as a whole, Article 6 'Our Infinite Universe' establishing infiniteness and Article 9 'Interconnectedness in an Infinite Universe' establishing interconnectedness, also apply to the universe as a whole and these three in conjunction seem to indicate that the universe is spatially symmetric.

The universe may be all that there is but the import of this would be lost without the conscious mind perceiving it as such. At best this perception is only partial; certain phenomena can only be understood probabilistically, not absolutely, although if the universe is indeed cyclic and like some complex clock-work, nothing in it is actually probabilistic.

Nothing better illustrates the power of intuitionism than the intuitive proof of the Continuum Hypothesis in Article 14 which necessitated an intuitive resolution of the set theoretic paradoxes. Mathematicians who were sensitive to the elegance and universality of intuitive mathematics regarded axiomatic systems (formal systems that supposedly side-stepped the paradoxes) as provisional solutions; the need for intuitionism was ever present, only the problems seemed insurmountable.

Certain metaphysical problems arise when familiar concepts are overly generalised, for example, the concept of 'nothing'. The 'nothing' that we use in everyday language cannot be extended to incorporate 'absolute nothing' of which we have no experience whatsoever. It is this over-extension that gives rise to the metaphysical riddle that seeks to understand why the universe 'bothered to exist'.

Certain other metaphysical problems arise when the wording of the problem itself is misleadingly suggestive. For example, the question 'Why Is the Universe the Way It Is?' in Article 4 may suggest it could have been otherwise, whereas this is impossible: it is forced to be what it in fact is.

With regard to the nature of matter, a central question has been its divisibility. The atomic view of matter that finally settled this question was a long time in coming, but it was based on experimental evidence, whereas Article 11 (i) 'On the Impossibility of Indefinite Reducibility of Matter' settles the issue by *á priori* reasoning.

Article 13 'Think You Know Your Own Mind?' reveals the limits of predictability and permits the observation that although predictability implies determinism, the converse is not true, that is, determinism does not imply predictability.

Although the universe is totally objective, the intentionality in conscious beings like us is totally subjective and so prose can never do full justice to 'happiness' or 'love', our most ardent desires, which can only be experienced or communicated poetically.

Contents

1   The Search for the Ultimate Truth 1

2   Physics and Metaphysics; Mathematics and

     Metamathematics 5

3   Why the Universe Bothered to Exist 9

4   Why Is the Universe the Way It Is? 11

5   (i) The Beginning of Time? 13

     (ii) An 'Open-ended' Journey without any Beginning? 15

     (iii) Our Cyclical Universe 17

     (iv) The Objective Nature of Cyclical Time 19

     (v) An Important Implication of Cyclicity Pertaining

     to the Scope of Artificial Intelligence 20

6   Our Infinite Universe 21

7   Determinism 23

8   Does There Exist Another 'Universe'? 29

9   Interconnectedness in an Infinite Universe 31

10   A Model for Our Universe 33

11   (i) On the Impossibility of Indefinite Reducibility of

     Matter 37

     (ii) Thomson's Lamp 40

12 Consciousness 43

13 Think You Know Your Own Mind? 47

14 An Intuitionistic Solution of the Continuum
    Hypothesis for Definable Sets and Resolution of the
    Set Theoretic Paradoxes 49

    Part I: The Continuum Hypothesis 52

    Part II: The Paradoxes 69

    Part III: Implications for Continuum Hypothesis on
    Account of Axiom of Choice 83

15 The Search for Happiness 85

16 The Song of Love 87

17 God 89

1

The Search for the Ultimate Truth

If we believe that there is something like ultimate reality, we already know something about it. Ask someone to explain more however and the mystery would probably only deepen. There is something out there in the vastness of space and time that is at the same time the cause and effect of all material phenomena and all sense experience, but what it is we cannot tell.

Who are we? Are we free? How are living things fundamentally different from non-living things? What is consciousness? Can we ever hope to understand it? Did the universe have to exist? Did it have a beginning? Why couldn't the universe have been different from what it in fact is? Is the universe finite or infinite? How many independent universes exist?

It needed a lot of introspection to even pose these age-old questions but try as they might, philosophers failed to come up with any universally acceptable solutions. Philosophy today is naive and in a state of disrepute. In comparison, science has proved itself time and again. We must remember, however, that science has never come up with universally acceptable solutions to the fundamental metaphysical questions and never will because science is essentially *á posteriori* and not *á priori* whereas the human soul thirsts for *á priori* enlightenment. Spiritual leaders and religious reformers have only succeeded in shifting the focus from nature to God, but both are one and the same. Both are omniscient, omnipotent and unique.

So does all this imply that the ultimate questions will remain shrouded in mystery forever? Alternatively, that they will entail a long, long search and finally only be comprehensively understood by a small handful?

In 'The Song of Zarathustra'[1], Friedrich Nietzsche suggests that time is circular rather than linear. His concept of 'eternal recurrence' is that everything that is happening now has already happened infinitely many times over in the past and will continue happening infinitely many times in the future in identical cycles!

Several *á priori* arguments seemingly endorse Nietzsche's revolutionary concept and these will be presented soon.

---

[1] Will Durant, *The Story of Philosophy*, Pocket Books: 2nd Edition, Chapter IX, Friedrich Nietzsche, Article IV, Page 413

One of the most fundamental aspects of nature is that it 'knows itself' and is 'its own justification'. Certain Jewish philosophers perceived this vaguely and speculated that 'God and His intellect and the things conceived by His intellect were one and the same thing'[2]. We may interpret and rephrase this, our cornerstone intuition/axiom (the non-arbitrariness Ultimate Reality law), as 'everything happens for a reason; nothing is arbitrary, superfluous or redundant in the universe'. We will dwell more on this later, but for now it will suffice to point out that a supposed beginning of time would preclude the universe from being its own justification, since at the supposed beginning it would already have evolved and come into being before it could possibly know what form to evolve to!

---

[2] Will Durant, *The Story of Philosophy*, Pocket Books: 2nd Edition Chapter IV, Spinoza, Article IV, 2 Matter and Mind, Page 176

2

Physics and Metaphysics;
Mathematics and Metamathematics

Physics proposes theories and assesses these in the light of observational evidence. The deficiency of this approach is that phenomena beyond observational range are not taken into account in the formulation of theories. It might seem worthless and impossible to take the non-observables into account but in fact this is not so.

Metaphysics comes into its own here. It is concerned with the basic nature of reality and combines intuition with accepted scientific theories to provide a unified view of nature.

The metaphysical results that will follow whilst being in conformity to those of physical science, will go much further than the latter and provide some simple yet compelling solutions to the age-old metaphysical mysteries.

Surprisingly, there also exist certain foundational issues in mathematics that can only be resolved 'metamathematically', that is, by intuitive insight in conjunction with formal proof.

The conjecture known as the 'Continuum Hypothesis' (CH) proposed by the mathematician Georg Cantor in the late 19th century was considered the most famous unsolved problem in mathematics. It is an example of a problem that was eventually solved only in an axiomatic framework and never in the originally intended intuitive framework.

Cantor proposed CH in the context of seeking the distinguishing feature of continuity. However the demise of intuitionism in mathematics following the discovery of the set theoretic paradoxes, gave rise to the axiomatization of set theory, which could not identify any distinguishing feature as envisaged by Cantor, continuity being an intuitive concept.

A formal proof of CH for all intuitively definable sets will be presented later and this will also enable identifying the distinguishing feature of continuity.

A prerequisite to reverting to intuitionistic set theory is the resolution of the set theoretic paradoxes, so a separate analysis of the paradoxes will address this.

The wide applicability of the intuitionistic method as exemplified in the forthcoming articles gives credence to this approach.

3

Why the Universe Bothered to Exist

The search for 'ultimate truth' essentially seeks an answer to two fundamental questions:

(i.) Why did the universe bother to exist?

(ii.) Why is the universe what it in fact is?

The former of these two was famously posed by Stephen Hawking in his acclaimed book, *A Brief History of Time*. The answer to this question would be "the ultimate triumph of human reason – for then we would know the mind of God"[3], states Hawking in his concluding lines.

What is in our nature that so yearns for an answer to these large and overwhelming questions, these questions that are almost

---

[3] Stephen Hawking, *A Brief History of Time: From the Big Bang to Black Holes*, New York: Bantam Books 1989, Page 185

spiritual in nature? More importantly, however, what form could any plausible answers have?

In a way, an adequate answer to the second question would also answer the first, for then the universe would be so compelling as to ensure its own existence. Here, however, we limit our discussion to directly answer the first question alone.

Why, indeed, did the universe bother to exist? Why couldn't it have remained 'nothing'? In order to answer this, we need to first examine what the alternative to existence – 'nothing' – means. While the common usage of the word suggests the absence of 'thing' in a given space, in the current context, 'nothing' is used in a unique abstract sense that is unimaginable in sense experience. Etymologically, the very definition of 'nothing' as 'no-thing' pre-supposes 'thing' with which it is mutually incompatible. 'Nothing' is equivalent to 'no-thing' and the latter is meaningless unless first of all 'thing' is meaningful, but 'thing' can only be meaningful if it in fact exists, in which event 'nothing' being incompatible with 'thing' obviously cannot exist.

It seems that there's nothing like nothing!

4

Why Is the Universe the Way It Is?

Psychologically, this question wins for itself the tacit acceptance of one or more alternative systems that could potentially have been our universe, when in fact this is not so; our universe necessarily had to be what it is.

Why so?

The reason is that whatever else our universe could or could not have been, it would necessarily have to be rich enough to contain the puzzle posed by the title question, since the puzzle presupposes its own existence.

It does not seem imperative for the universe to contain a particular tree or a particular rock, or for that matter, any particular thing, except the puzzle itself; it _is_ imperative that the universe contain the puzzle, for the puzzle to be solved at all, and if this is so, the universe could be conceived as that <u>unique</u> design that contains the puzzle: the puzzle cannot exist in isolation, all by itself, it necessarily has to have a 'supporting structure'; for the puzzle to exist, we need to exist, our planet needs to exist..., our universe needs to exist.

Why unique?

The answer is that were it possible for other designs to contain the puzzle, the design actually adopted by nature to represent the universe would be arbitrary but our 'non-arbitrariness' axiom (page 3) prohibits arbitrariness.

5

(i) The Beginning of Time?

Time could either be beginningless or have had a beginning.

Although the idea of God as a creator might necessitate time to have a beginning and for different reasons, so would the Big Bang theory of the universe, *á priori* reasoning does <u>not</u> support this view, principally because a beginning in time poses unsolvable conceptual difficulties with respect to the initial conditions. Einstein himself was perplexed when he wondered whether God had any freedom in choosing the initial conditions and Stephen Hawking expressed his wonderment for this when he famously posed the question as to why the universe 'bothered to exist'. The truth is that if the universe indeed had a beginning, these questions would be intrinsically inexplicable.

The supposed beginning of time in the Big Bang theory of the universe seemingly suggests that time did indeed have a beginning, but this 'beginning' should be interpreted as that point in the past when empirical physical theories break down, rather than literally as some beginning of time.

Again, if 'beginning' be conceptualised as 'nothing before', we would be confronted with the incongruity of 'something coming from nothing'.

Also, hypothetical beginnings would not only fail to explain the initial conditions, that is, the initial instantaneous values of time-dependent variables, but also fail in the endeavour to conceptualise these initial instantaneous values. This is so since such conceptualisations necessarily rely on nature's past, which is non-existent in the event of a beginning. For example, initial instantaneous velocity cannot even be conceived if the past is not taken into account. Even though mathematically speaking it is possible to associate a supposed initial instantaneous velocity with its future effects, its philosophical conceptualisation necessarily has to be independent of the future since a value for it is presumed to exist prior to the future.

We conclude that time is without beginning and is necessarily beginningless.

(ii) An 'Open-ended' Journey without any Beginning?

Imagine a car travelling strictly from left to right at a constant speed, say 100 m.p.h., along a straight road stretching from 'minus infinity' to 'plus infinity'. Suppose the car has been travelling since time immemorial, so there is no beginning point for its journey: it is beginningless!

Were there to be positioned milestones at intervals of one mile each all along the road, the road being infinite, there would be infinite milestones and these could have markings '1' '2' '3' … *ad. infinitum* on the right side of a milestone marked '0' and sequentially '–1', '–2', '–3' … *ad. infinitum.* on the left side of the '0' milestone thus:

$$… -3, -2, -1, 0, 1, 2, 3 …$$

Question: Is such a beginningless journey possible?

Answer: It might seem possible but in fact it is impossible.

This is so, since were it possible, we could then very well imagine another car simultaneously travelling once again at a constant speed of 100 m.p.h. but this time strictly from right to left in its beginningless journey.

In a thought experiment such as this, the two cars would be expected to meet at some 'mid-way' point, but the stretch 'minus infinity' to 'plus infinity' has no 'mid-way' point. (It is fallacious to think that the mid-way point coincides with the position of the '0' milestone since this milestone can very well be positioned at any arbitrary location on the infinite stretch 'minus infinity' to 'plus infinity'). In fact there isn't any preferred meeting point on the infinite stretch although there should be a preferred meeting point since all variables in the thought experiment are explicit.

This proves the impossibility of any such beginningless 'open-ended' journey wherein the limit points 'minus infinity' and 'plus infinity' are distinct from each other.

The only alternative beginningless journey is one that is not open-ended but rather along some closed loop. (A piece of string can either have its ends joined, in which case, if the string represents the flow of time, time would be cyclic; alternatively, the two ends of the string could be disjoint, that is, open-ended, which would represent linear time).

(iii) Our Cyclical Universe

With reference to the evolution of our own universe, Article 5 (i) (The Beginning of Time?) established beginninglessness and Article 5 (ii) (An Open-ended Journey Without Any Beginning?) analogously suggests that it could never have 'open-endedly' evolved from an infinite past to its present state, an absurd 'infinite process', so, it would necessarily be within a closed time loop, that is, the universe would be cyclic[4].

If time is cyclic, the compulsive repetitiousness inherent in cyclicity is constraint enough to assure some particular forced evolution of the universe. The universe then <u>necessarily</u> evolves the way it does. On the other hand, were time to be open-ended, there is no necessity for the universe to evolve the way it does.

---

[4] Adam, John et al., *The Science Book: Big Ideas Simply Explained* (Dorling Kindersley Limited, 2014) Gabriele Veneziano, A Theory of Everything, Page 312
"Superstring theory predicts the existence of multidimensional branes. Our universe might be one such brane. It is suggested that a Big Bang event occurs when two branes collide producing a "Cyclic Universe" model." (For further reading)

Let us illustrate this with a simple example. Consider some finite or infinite sequence of natural numbers, representing the states of the universe. Even if the sequence is in accordance with some identifiable pattern, there is no assurance of the pattern's continuance; the pattern could very well cease at any instant, unlike the case where time is cyclic!

So if we believe that the universe does not evolve arbitrarily or alternatively that it necessarily evolves the way it does (both being the same thing), the universe would have to be cyclic.

Cyclicity ultimately explains why nature behaves as it does: it is always <u>forced</u> to go by precedent and precedent always exists by virtue of cyclicity and the question as to who or what set the precedent does not arise when time is without beginning or end.

(iv) The Objective Nature of Cyclical Time

While scientists' conceptions of physical entities are inextricably linked to the measurability of those entities, intuitive notions of the same entities may <u>not</u> be so linked.

For example, 'cyclic-time', the time-duration of one cycle, is seemingly independent of its measurability and hence can be considered objective and not subjective and this distinction is important to avoid unnecessary controversy regarding its measurability.

(v) An Important Implication of Cyclicity Pertaining to the Scope of Artificial Intelligence

The central philosophical problem here is whether or not artificial intelligence can ever replicate the thinking of conscious beings.

The simple answer is 'no'.

This is so since although cyclicity implies strict determinism, this is not so in physical science, an incomplete description of nature in which evolution is probabilistic rather than deterministic, so there is an unbridgeable gap between all the knowledge we can ever have and all that actually exists and in particular, consciousness, being outside the scope of physical science, can never be artificially replicated.

6

Our Infinite Universe

When we think of space, we think of a boundless extension that supposedly contains everything (our universe).

Dimensionally, the universe can either be bounded (finite) or unbounded and if unbounded it can either be unbounded over the continuum of time or unbounded all at once (infinite). This article will only prove that the universe cannot be bounded but in conjunction with Article 5 (iii) (Our Cyclical Universe), the universe would have to be unbounded all at once (infinite), since the alternative unbounded expansion is ruled out by the cyclicity constraint.

Were the universe to be bounded, a pictorial depiction of it could be visualised as, say, an orange disc of finite size within a black background representing 'nothing' (the boundless extension); however, since 'nothing' cannot be represented, a finite universe is untenable.

On the one hand we feel compelled to visualize a background in any finite depiction of the universe, on the other hand this 'background' is a meaningless concept since it is totally unrelated to any other accepted concept, in the sense it makes no difference to our hypothetical finite universe whether the background is affirmed or denied.

7

Determinism

The philosophical doctrine of determinism has been intensely debated, yet opinion is divided as to its truth or falsity. The odd thing is that the absence of a coherent definition of determinism was not a deterrent in the pursuit of a conclusion on this matter.

The dictionary definition[5] that determinism is the 'inevitable consequence of antecedents' and is 'independent of human will', although essentially correct, is not powerful enough to distinguish determinism from indeterminism. Science's linking determinism with predictability is also not justifiable. Yes, predictability implies determinism, but the converse is not true; determinism does not imply predictability.

---

[5] *Reader's Digest Universal Dictionary*, 1988, s.v. "determinism" The philosophical doctrine that every event, act, and decision is the inevitable consequence of antecedents, such as physical, psychological, or environmental conditions, that are independent of the individual human will.

Predictability seemed a natural criterion for determinism since it was felt that nature could only be deterministic if its evolution uniquely proceeded according to natural laws assumed (fallaciously) to be knowable. Then, when quantum theory debunked knowability, it was felt that nature was indeterministic.

However, we can prove determinism by virtue of Article 5 (iii) (Our Cyclical Universe) that establishes the cyclic nature of time and cyclicity not only ensures determinism but is also the one and only elusive metaphysical criterion that unambiguously distinguishes determinism from indeterminism.

An interesting paradox 'The Kid's Dilemma' concerning determinism will now be presented.

Rashu, a 7-year-old philosophical yet playful kid has to prepare for an examination the following day, but reasons with his mother to allow him to while away the evening playing table tennis.

Rashu: (smiles) Ma, can I go and play T.T.?

Ma: (frowns) And your exam?

Rashu: If it's determined that I'll pass, I'll pass and if it's determined that I'll fail, I'll fail.

Ma: (amused) Nonsense dear.

<u>Rashu</u>: (seriously) Why, Ma? Don't you believe in God?

<u>Ma</u>: Of course I do, but what's that got to do with it?

<u>Rashu</u>: Ma, if I could take a look at God's book of complete knowledge, it would be either 'pass' or 'fail' for me and nothing I do could change that outcome, so in either case, I need not study.

<u>Ma</u>: But how can you possibly look at His book? Surely God wouldn't want you to see it!

<u>Rashu</u>: (patiently) Ma, I was going to explain that even without actually seeing it, I need not study by my earlier logic.

<u>Ma</u>: (confidently) You're wrong, my son, but your reasoning is nevertheless laudable. It makes all the difference whether you actually see His book or not. Your reasoning would have been fool proof were you to actually see His book, but falls apart when you don't in fact know the outcome of your exam. Let's break up your thought process: you imply (i) if in God's book it is *pass*, you need not study and likewise (ii) if in God's book it is *fail*, you need not study. However, seen individually, each is illogical. For example, consider (i): the operative word here is 'if', implying that you do not know—you cannot avoid studying just because you *may* pass. You similarly cannot avoid studying because you *may* fail. Suppose, for example, God/determinism intended you to pass but also intended you to study. Then, since seeing His book

could dissuade you from studying, God cannot permit you to see the book!

Rashu: (resignedly) O.K. Ma, I guess I'll play T.T. some other day.

In the dictionary definition of determinism, 'psychological antecedents' are also mentioned. Does this imply that independent of the physical configuration of the universe, there exists something else that determines the universe's evolution?

Answer: No, nothing else.

In that case does it mean that consciousness has no role in the physical evolution of the universe?

Answer: It does not mean that consciousness has no role. Were consciousness not taken into account, the physical evolution would not be determined to be what it in fact is.

But are not the above two answers contradictory?

Answer: No, since consciousness can be considered an attribute that necessarily arises in beings that embody the requisite physical (atomic) configuration.

But this yet raises the question as to why nature deemed it necessary to have consciousness at all.

Answer: Beings like us being basically feedback and control systems, need signals regarding our state of well-being, but with physical science considering these as 'indeterminate systems', such feedback signals are impossible. It requires something outside of physical science for signalling to be at all possible and consciousness is that something.

8

Does There Exist Another 'Universe'?

Nomenclature for this article:

U_1 ... the cluster that we refer to as 'our universe' comprising a self-contained system of interacting particles.

U_2 ... a hypothetical cluster supposedly distinct and totally independent of U_1.

The issue to be resolved now is whether or not U_2, the supposed 'other' universe, exists.

It is impossible to either affirm or deny the existence of U_2 on purely scientific grounds since U_2 being totally independent of U_1, no observational confirmation of its existence would be possible.

However there exists a noteworthy metaphysical argument that rules out U_2's existence. This argument relies on the 'non-arbitrariness' Ultimate Reality law (page 3) asserting that nothing whatsoever in the universe is arbitrary.

Consider the cluster U_1. Since this is the one and only independent and self-contained cluster in our experience, there is no reason that it cannot represent nature in all its totality. This implies that it is not necessary that U_2 exist, so if nature is *á priorily* necessarily what it in fact is and not arbitrary, U_2 cannot exist.

Hypothetically if for some reason U_1 cannot represent nature in all its totality and U_2 necessarily has to exist, it implies that there <u>has</u> to be a connection/relation between U_1 and U_2, which is impossible, U_2 supposedly being totally independent of U_1.

9

Interconnectedness in
an Infinite Universe

Article 6 (Our Infinite Universe) gave a metaphysical proof that our universe is infinite and Article 8 (Does there Exist another 'Universe'?) denied the existence of another universe.

These two articles in conjunction give an interesting result. This is that our infinite universe cannot possibly be composed of sub-systems that are totally independent of each other at all times; all such sub-systems are interconnected.

To prove this, suppose the contrary, that is our infinite universe, say 'I', is composed of two independent clusters 'U_1' and 'U_2' and we inhabit U_1. Then the current article forces us to accept the existence of U_2 whereas Article 8 prohibits U_2's existence, which is a contradiction; so the clusters U_1 and U_2 cannot be independent at all times and rather are interconnected.

10

A Model for Our Universe

Our universe is a system with certain unique features. It is the one and only system that can exist independently. Also, it is infinite in spatial extent (Article 6) and cyclic in time (Article 5 (iii)).

Since space is conceptualised in terms of its contents, the contents in the universe necessarily extend over a boundless extension and are not confined to any bounded spatial region.

Article 9 (Interconnectedness in an Infinite Universe) proves that our infinite universe cannot possibly be composed of two or more sub-systems that are totally independent of each other. The model for our infinite universe that will be proposed in this article will primarily be constrained by the twin constraints of this inter-connectedness of the universe's sub-systems and its characteristic of cyclicity in time.

The very 'reason' for the universe's existence in Article 3 (Why the Universe Bothered to Exist) reveals the purely metaphysical nature of this inquiry.

The foregoing indicates that:

1. The universe necessarily exists
2. It is not arbitrary
3. It is infinite
4. It is cyclic, and
5. It is interconnected

These five laws derived from purely *á priori* reasoning will henceforth be referred to as the 'Ultimate Reality' (UR) laws.

We may identify yet another markedly different independent UR law (the 6th UR law). This is the law asserting the primacy of consciousness/thought. It is this law that is used for answering the question 'why is the universe what it in fact is'. Whatever the universe is or is not, it is necessary to assume that it is rich enough to include the quoted question if at all this question needs to be resolved, but the quotation obviously presupposes thought/consciousness.

The UR laws are necessary but not sufficient to yield a unique model of the universe. Also the cyclicity UR law imposes strict limitations on the possible models for the universe. Any such model needs to be extremely precisely structured, even unimaginably so, and it is likely that such precise structuring can only be achieved in a spatially symmetric model.

It is possible to envisage the desired model as one possessing infinite 'sources' and 'sinks' symmetrically juxtaposed such that sources' eruptions of matter are absorbed by neighbouring sinks which in turn after some saturation level themselves become sources whilst the previous sources, being considerably depleted on account of the eruptions, now become sinks.

This model seemingly satisfies our five UR laws.

11

(i) On the Impossibility of Indefinite Reducibility of Matter

Is matter indefinitely reducible to smaller and yet smaller components without limit or is there a limit?

Physicists believe that there is a limit and the smallest units of matter are the subatomic particles.

In this article, we prove by *á priori* reasoning that there is indeed a limit to reducibility, beyond which further sub-division of matter is impossible.

Consider a dowel rod, say one meter long, and assume that its ends are marked '0' and '1' respectively. Let us see whether we can go on and on dividing it, without limit.

Suppose, for argument's sake, that we can in fact imagine it to be divided into infinite pieces. The first division could be at the half-way mark, that is, $\frac{1}{2}$ meter from 0 and the piece from 0 to $\frac{1}{2}$ $\left(0 \cdot \frac{1}{2}\right)$ could be imagined to be detached from the remainder of the rod and kept aside.

Next, the remainder of the rod, that is, from $\frac{1}{2}$ metre to 1 metre $\left(\frac{1}{2} \cdot 1\right)$ could in turn be divided in half by a division at $\frac{3}{4}$ metre away from 0 and the piece $\left(\frac{1}{2} \cdot \frac{3}{4}\right)$ could be imagined to be detached and kept aside.

Proceeding thus, each remaining piece could be divided into half, the first half imagined to be set aside and the second half in turn divided into half, so that the pieces imagined to be detached would be $\left(0 \cdot \frac{1}{2}\right)$, $\left(\frac{1}{2} \cdot \frac{3}{4}\right)$, $\left(\frac{3}{4} \cdot \frac{7}{8}\right)$. . . *ad infinitum.*

It can be seen that the pieces progressively get smaller and smaller without limit and an infinite number of pieces can be imagined to be detached in this way.

Question: Do the infinite detached pieces make up the full rod?

Answer: Yes and no! 'Yes' because whenever a rod is divided into any number of pieces, all the pieces <u>do</u> make up the original rod; 'no' because the mark '1' on the rod does not appear in a single one of the detached pieces.

Conclusion: An answer that is both a 'yes' as well as a 'no' is obviously contradictory and this contradiction arose only because of the supposition that the rod could be indefinitely divided. This implies that the rod (or any material object in general) can never be divided into pieces less than some particular size, which could be considered the smallest unit of length in nature.

(ii) Thomson's Lamp

The ideas espoused in the present article have relevance in considerations of the feasibility of 'infinite-task' machines in general, that is, machines capable of performing infinite tasks in a finite time.

Notwithstanding considerable research in this subject, deep-seated conceptual issues have hitherto remained unresolved.

As a particular example, consider 'Thomson's Lamp'[6]. This magic lamp goes on and off alternately during a time period of 1 minute; it is 'on' for $\frac{1}{2}$ a minute, then 'off' for $\frac{1}{4}$ of a minute, 'on' for $\frac{1}{8}$ of a minute, 'off' for $\frac{1}{16}$ of a minute, and so on, an infinite number of times in 1 minute. The question now is: will the lamp be 'on' or 'off' at precisely 1 minute from start?

Intuitively, the answer should depend on whether it started with an 'on' or 'off'. However, in this way, were the $\frac{1}{2}$ minute 'on' start to be disregarded and the $\frac{1}{4}$ minute 'off' in fact regarded as the

---

[6] John D. Barrow, *The Infinite Book: A Short Guide to the Boundless, Timeless and Endless* (Jonathan Cape, London 2005) Chapter 10 Making Infinity Machines: Rubbing Thomson's Lamp Page 218

new 'start', a different answer to the question would ensue! An impossibility. This implies that it cannot be said whether the lamp is 'on' or 'off' at the 1 minute mark, it is 'indeterminate'.

But how can this be? Of course, the limiting speed of the on/off switchings being infinite, practically speaking, Thomson's Lamp cannot function as described. This however does not detract from the conceptual hurdle of the 'end-game' problem: how would the on/off 'process' end?

Answer: The on/off process depicted is actually an example of an *infinite step in finite time process* that is essentially 'endless' in the sense that it cannot be said to terminate at any definite moment of time. In particular, it does <u>not</u> terminate at 1 minute, the 1 minute time-mark being only a limit point (earliest stop-point) of the process that is <u>not</u> a point of the process time! This is so since although the sum of the infinite geometric series $\frac{1}{2} + \frac{1}{4} + \frac{1}{8} + \frac{1}{16} + \ldots$ *ad inf.* is precisely 1, the time intervals $\frac{1}{2}, \frac{1}{4}, \frac{1}{8}, \frac{1}{16} \ldots$ *ad inf.* cumulatively do <u>not</u> include the 1 minute time-mark, this mark not appearing in any of these intervals.

Note: A lamp that functions like Thomson's Lamp is logically conceivable if and only if in addition to it's on/off process extending over 1 minute, it's on/off status at precisely the 1-minute mark is assumed to be in accordance with some prior explicitly stipulated specification. Otherwise, on the one hand, the lamp's on/off status would be indeterminate but on the other hand it is forced to be either on or off, which is inconceivable.

Comments: In this article and Article 11 (i) 'On the Impossibility of Indefinite Reducibility of Matter', the 1-mark is excluded, it representing distance in 11 (i) and time in 11 (ii).

12

Consciousness

Consciousness, our rich inner world of sensations, feelings and meanings, necessarily arises whenever the physical structure embodying it comes into being.

Consciousness is a fundamental concept. Only our direct experience of it convinces us of its existence: it cannot be derived from physical science. Yet, consciousness is not magic. It is just that it is beyond science, which itself is a natural process with hitherto unimaginable limitations.

Scientific knowledge alone is obviously inadequate to understand what the conscious being experiences, but this should not have been were science a complete description of nature, which it is not. Again, had science understood nature in all its totality, consciousness would have been redundant, science's 'understanding' excluding as it does sensation and feeling; however, by virtue of the non-arbitrariness UR law (page 3), this cannot be since nature is neither arbitrary nor superfluous.

Philosophers find consciousness mysterious because physical and computational theories of brain function do not incorporate consciousness at all, but this is to be expected, consciousness lying outside the scope of science. Yes, the conscious mind is like a computer, but one whose software will remain hidden forever, relying as it does on intangible consciousness.

So it seems the conscious mind actively influences action. But how? It seems impossible to explain how the intangible conscious mind can interact with tangible matter. How can intangible thought will the tangible physical body to act? This, the 'mind-matter paradox', only arises if the external physiochemical transformations and the internal ones of the conscious mind are viewed as two separate, distinct processes, which they in fact are not. They are to be viewed as but one process—neither is the cause or effect of the other—so the question of interaction of mind and matter does not arise.

The nature of the subjective experience with respect to conscious decision is 'feeling', the 'gap' between the 'desired' physiochemical state and the 'occurring' physiochemical state of the being. The feeling is the trigger for a sequence of conscious processes involving memory and analysis and culminating in intentionality.

In a way, consciousness can be considered an emergent phenomenon. This is so since beings like us can be thought of as a particular class of indeterministic systems which evolve probabilistically rather than uniquely in physical science. However by virtue of Article 5 (iii) (Our Cyclical Universe), this is false. Our thoughts and actions are deterministic, not probabilistic. These conflicting views can only be reconciled if it is acknowledged that physical science is an incomplete description of nature and that there exist concepts outside its scope, which in conjunction with it, allow a unique evolution of such systems. Consciousness is one such concept.

13

Think You Know Your Own Mind?

We who desire to understand our universe seemingly cannot even understand our own minds! A thought experiment will clarify what is meant by this. Think of any trivial thing that you would not do without some compelling reason, for example, standing on the tip of your toes, stretching your arm upwards and touching the ceiling. Now ask yourself if you can ascertain whether or not you would do this in the next five minutes for no reason whatsoever.

Your first reaction could be to assert that you would refrain: you would know that in the absence of any compelling reason, you would certainly not touch the ceiling.

Now since knowing anything with certainty is equivalent to considering the opposite of that thing an impossibility, it implies that you consider touching the ceiling without any reason an impossibility, which is absurd; so it seems that if you think you know, then you do not know!

Were you to accept the foregoing argument, you could reflect some more and then decide that in fact you do not know or are not sure whether or not you would touch that ceiling. But alas, one could then argue that if you did not know then surely you would not touch the ceiling without reason, so in fact you would know!

Thought apparently breaks down if the thing is trivial enough and it is impossible for us to predict our own behaviour. If so, we should not be too surprised if we are unable to predict certain other natural phenomena as well. It is important to note, however, that if something is inherently unpredictable, it does not mean it is necessarily arbitrary and in fact, in Article 7 (Determinism), we identified a unique criterion for deterministic systems that holds for our universe.

14

An Intuitionistic Solution of the Continuum Hypothesis for Definable Sets and Resolution of the Set Theoretic Paradoxes

About the paper

The paper that follows consists essentially of a solution of the Continuum Hypothesis for all sets which can intuitively be considered definable, with the section on paradoxes justifying its intuitive basis.

The Continuum Hypothesis was for long regarded the most famous unsolved problem in mathematics. Subsequently in 1963, the works of Gödel and Cohen proved the independence of the Continuum Hypothesis within the framework of an <u>axiomatic set theory</u>.

The paper, however, proves the Continuum Hypothesis for all definable sets within the framework of classical intuitive set theory which can arguably be considered the mathematical theory in which mathematicians originally sought a solution of the Continuum Hypothesis: a theory that is both all-encompassing in its generality and beautiful in its simplicity.

Unfortunately, classical intuitive set theory was abandoned by mathematicians years ago in favour of several axiomatic set theories. This was primarily to side-step the apparent inconsistencies of classical intuitive set theory as manifested by the set theoretic paradoxes. Now since this paper basically reaffirms the stand of classical intuitive set theory, it was imperative to 'resolve' the set theoretic paradoxes to justify the intuitive approach in the first place. Also, since the solution of the Continuum Hypothesis entailed the use of concepts such as 'specifiable' or 'definable' real number and its counterpart 'unspecifiable' or 'undefinable' real number, it was necessary to resolve certain fundamental questions posed by Richard's paradox in particular and other set theoretic paradoxes in general.

It can be appreciated that the subject matter of the paper, strewn as it is with paradoxical concepts, requires very sharp analytical distinctions and a very fundamental grasp of the intricacies. A sort of 'quantum logic' is also involved. The approach and ideas of the paper however are fairly straightforward and expounded with all the rigour of traditional classical intuitive mathematics.

Although the ideas are succinctly expounded, the paper's format is necessarily non-standard since current research in classical intuitive set theory is virtually non-existent for the reasons mentioned and in particular, no standard format was ever developed to expound the quantum logical ideas contained in this paper which both solves the age old problem of the Continuum Hypothesis and simultaneously reaffirms classical intuitive set theory.

Part I: The Continuum Hypothesis

1. <u>Introduction</u>: This paper has three parts. Part I consists of an intuitive proof of the Continuum Hypothesis (CH) for all definable sets. Part II is a systematic treatment of the set theoretic paradoxes and is complementary to Part I: it justifies the intuitive approach adopted in Part I notwithstanding the problems posed by the paradoxes and it reveals that the scope of Part I extends to include all 'definable' sets – even the 'paradoxical' ones! Part III, an addendum to parts I and II, argues that CH is undecidable if the Axiom of Choice (AC) is included in the set of axioms of typical axiomatic set theories.

The arguments involving as they do sets of real numbers, it is necessary now to dwell on certain fundamental concepts associated with real numbers and their sets.

A fundamental concept associated with real numbers is that of 'characteristic property' (CP), which is any finitely describable property that is 'meaningful' (true or false) for each real number. Thus for example, the property 'is a rational number', being finitely describable and meaningful for each real number, is a CP of real numbers.

A CP can also be used as a 'defining property' (DP) to define the set of all real numbers possessing that property. For example, the same CP mentioned above can be used as a DP to define the set of all rational numbers {x | x is a rational number}. In fact, it can be seen that corresponding to each CP, there exists a definable set that has that CP as its DP.

Another fundamental concept is that of 'general negation' of a CP, which as its name suggests is that CP obtained by inserting the word 'not' at the appropriate place in a given CP so as to get the 'opposite' of that CP. For example, 'is <u>not</u> a rational number' is the general negation of 'is a rational number' and vice-versa. For convenience, such pairs of CPs wherein each is the general negation of the other, will be referred to as 'mutually repellent' pairs of CPs.

A crucial concept is that of a 'specifiable' real number, which simply speaking is any finitely describable real number. Its counterpart, an 'unspecifiable' real number, is any real number that is <u>not</u> a specifiable. (The corollary to Proposition (3) below asserts the existence of an unspecifiable real number).

Two elementary propositions concerning specifiable real numbers now follow.

2. <u>Proposition</u>: Any infinite definable set S consisting exclusively of specifiable real numbers is denumerable.

<u>Proof</u>: Each element of S, being specifiable, can be expressed by a finite expression of the English language and the set of all such expressions is denumerable; an enumeration can be given for example by specifying that expression E_i precedes E_j if E_i contains fewer symbols than E_j and if they contain the same number of symbols, precedence is determined by lexicographic ordering; the symbols being alphabetical letters, punctuation marks and the blank space between words (which will also be treated as a symbol).

3. <u>Proposition</u>: All real numbers are not specifiable.

<u>Proof</u>: If all real numbers were specifiable, the set of all real numbers would be denumerable, which it is not.

<u>Corollary</u>: There exists an unspecifiable real number.

We now state the Schroder – Bernstein theorem which will be used to deduce the corollary following it, which in turn will be used to prove proposition (7).

4. Schröder – Bernstein[7] theorem: For any pair of sets A and B, if A is equivalent to a subset of B and B is equivalent to a subset of A, then A is equivalent to B.

Corollary: If S is any set of real numbers and a subset of S is equivalent to the set of all real numbers, then S is equivalent to the set of all real numbers.

5. On 'complete' and 'partial' description of real numbers and the depiction of certain infinite sequences of CPs by means of an 'infinite branch': An arbitrary CP of real numbers segregates certain real numbers from the remaining ones and may be considered a 'complete' or 'partial' description of a real number accordingly as the CP segregates only one real number or more than one real number from the remaining real numbers. For example, descriptions like 'is π', 'is $\sqrt{2}$', 'is $\frac{3}{4}$', etc. are complete descriptions of real numbers, segregating as they do a single real number from the remaining ones. Comparatively, descriptions like 'is a rational number', 'is a solution of the algebraic equation $x^2 - 3x + 2 = 0$', 'is > 2', etc. are partial descriptions of real numbers.

Certainly, a description is either complete or partial and these categories are exhaustive and mutually exclusive.

---

[7] Seymour Lipschutz, *Theory and Problems of Set Theory and Related Topics* (Schaum's Outline Series, McGraw-Hill Book Co., 1964), Chapter 9, Page 140

In case a real number r is completely described by means of some description, say p, no further information about r can be given in the sense that for no CP C can it be said that 'C can possibly be considered as giving additional information about r, that is, information in addition to that given by p', since p being a complete description of r, each CP C of real numbers by its very definition is either true or false for r (either is a CP of r or not a CP of r) and in either case, such a CP cannot possibly be considered as giving additional information about r.

On the other hand if r is partially described, there necessarily exists a CP which can possibly be considered as giving additional information about r, since the contrary assumption that no such CP exists, implies that any arbitrary CP either is a CP of r or is not a CP of r, which implies that r is completely described, contrary to our assumption that it is not.

For example, if r is partially described by means of the partial description 'is a rational number', the CP 'is a real number in the open interval (0, 1)' can possibly be considered as giving additional information about r, as also the general negation of this CP, that is, 'is not a real number in the open interval (0, 1)'. In general it is true that the general negation of some particular CP which can possibly be considered as giving additional information about some real number r partially described by means of some partial description p, can also possibly be considered as giving additional information about r.

Now if C_1 denotes some CP that is in fact considered as giving additional information, the '1st additional bit of information', about a real number r partially described by some partial description p, C_1 in conjunction with p may or may not completely describe r. In the former case, that is, C_1 in conjunction with p completely describes r, no CP can possibly be considered as giving yet more information about r. Comparatively, in the latter case, that is, C_1 in conjunction with p only partially describes r, there necessarily exists yet another CP which can possibly be considered as giving yet more information, the '2nd additional bit of information', about r.

In general, we can say: 'if r denotes a particular real number partially described by means of some partial description p, there exists a CP which can possibly be considered as giving additional information, the '1st additional bit of information', about r and if C_1 denotes any particular such CP which is in fact considered as giving the 1st additional bit of information about r but which yet in conjunction with p leaves r partially described, there exists a 2nd CP which can possibly be considered as giving the 2nd additional bit of information about r and if C_2 denotes any particular such CP which is in fact considered as giving the 2nd additional bit of information about r but which yet in conjunction with C_1 and p leaves r partially described, there exists a 3rd CP which can possibly be considered as giving the 3rd additional bit of information about r … *ad inf.* … (A).

For example, if 'is a natural number' is considered to be the partial description p of a real number r, the CPs of the infinite sequence 'is an element of the set {1, 3, 5, … *ad inf.*}', 'is an element of the set {1, 5, 9, … *ad inf.*}', 'is an element of the set {1, 9, 17, *ad inf.*}', … *ad inf.* may be considered to be the C$_1$, C$_2$, C$_3$, … *ad inf.* respectively in (A). It can readily be seen that no finite consecutive CPs of this sequence starting with the first CP completely describes r, but all the CPs cumulatively taken completely describe r to be the natural number 1.

It is not necessarily so however that cumulatively taken, the CPs of such sequences completely describe r. For example, if 'is a natural number' is considered as some partial description p of a real number r and the CPs 'is an element of the set {1, 5, 9, … *ad inf.* and 2, 6, 10, … *ad inf.*}', 'is an element of the set {1, 9, 17, … *ad inf.*. and 2, 10, 18, … *ad inf.*}', 'is an element of the set {1, 17, 33, … *ad inf.* and 2, 18, 34, … *ad inf.*', …. *ad inf.* are considered to be the C$_1$, C$_2$, C$_3$, …. *ad inf.* respectively in (A), it can readily be seen that unlike the previous example wherein the CPs of the sequence cumulatively taken completely described r to be the natural number 1, here the CPs of the sequence cumulatively taken only partially describe r to be an element of the set {1, 2}.

It is worth noting here that even if an infinite sequence of CPs C_1, C_2, C_3, ... *ad inf.* is such that for any particular natural number n, however large, the first n consecutive CPs of the sequence starting with C_1 are such that C_1 can possibly be considered the 1st additional bit of information about r, C_2 can possibly be considered the 2nd additional bit of information about r, C_3 can possibly be considered the 3rd additional bit of information about r, ... C_n can possibly be considered the nth additional bit of information about r, it <u>does not</u> imply that the sequence is of the type defined in (A). For example, if p denotes 'is a natural number', the CP sequence 'is > 1', 'is > 2', 'is > 3', ... *ad inf.* <u>is</u> of the above mentioned type but not of the type defined in (A), since no natural number can possibly possess all the CPs of this sequence.

The infinite sequences of CPs of the type defined in (A) can be depicted by means of an 'infinite branch' thus: $C_1 \rightarrow C_2 \rightarrow C_3 \rightarrow$ ... *ad inf.*, wherein for each natural number n, the nth CP C_n can be conceived as one which can possibly be considered as giving the nth additional bit of information about r, that is, information in addition to that given by C_{n-1}, C_{n-2}, ... C_2, C_1 and p, and r can be conceived as one satisfying the partial description p and in addition possibly possessing all CPs of the infinite sequence cumulatively.

6. <u>Simultaneous depiction of a number of interrelated in-</u>
<u>finite sequences of CPs by means of an 'infinite tree-diagram'</u>:
Consider the statement: 'If r denotes a particular real number
partially described by means of some partial description p,
there exists a mutually repellent pair of CPs, either CP of which
can possibly be considered as giving the 1st additional bit of
information about r and if $<C_0, C_1>$ denotes any particular
such mutually repellent pair of CPs, either CP of this pair can in
fact be considered the 1st additional bit of information about r;
then if C_0 in conjunction with p yet leaves r partially described,
there exists a 2nd pair of mutually repellent CPs, either CP of
which can possibly be considered as giving the 2nd additional
bit of information about r and if $<C_{00}, C_{01}>$ denotes any particular such 2nd mutually repellent pair of CPs, either CP of this
pair can in fact be considered as giving the 2nd additional bit of
information about r, the 1st additional bit of information about
r being C_0; similarly if C_1 in conjunction with p yet leaves r partially described, there exists a 2nd pair of mutually repellent CPs,
either CP of which can possibly be considered as giving the 2nd
additional bit of information about r and if $<C_{10}, C_{11}>$ denotes
any particular such 2nd mutually repellent pair of CPs, either CP
of this pair can in fact be considered the 2nd additional bit of
information about r, the 1st additional bit of information about
r being C_1; ... *ad inf.'* ... (B).

This statement (B) involves infinite sequences of CPs of the form Ci_1, Ci_1i_2, ... $Ci_1i_2 ... i_n$, ... *ad inf.* wherein each of the subscript symbols i_1, i_2, ... i_n, ... *ad inf.* can assume the values 0 or 1, the value of any given subscript symbol in each CP in any given infinite sequence of CPs, remaining constant.

The infinite sequences of CPs may conveniently be depicted by means of an 'infinite tree-diagram' as follows:

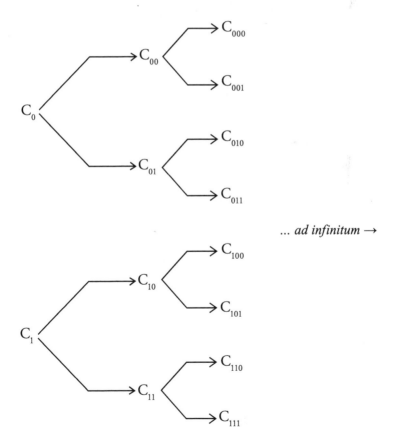

... ad infinitum →

A 'branch' of this diagram may be defined as any sequence of CPs (finite or infinite) starting with C_0 or C_1 such that any consecutive pair of CPs of the sequence are 'linked' by an arrow symbol of the diagram (occur just prior to the base and just after the tip respectively of an arrow symbol).

In terms of this nomenclature, it can readily be seen that the infinite sequences of CPs in statement (B) are precisely those depicted by infinite branches in the infinite tree-diagram and from the assumptions of this statement, the CP sequences in each infinite branch are like the CP sequence occurring in statement (A), in the sense that in each infinite branch of the infinite tree-diagram, the 1ˢᵗ CP of the infinite branch can possibly be considered as giving the 1ˢᵗ additional bit of information about r, the 2ⁿᵈ CP can possibly be considered as giving the 2ⁿᵈ additional bit of information about r, the 3ʳᵈ CP can possibly be considered as giving the 3ʳᵈ additional bit of information about r ... *ad inf.*

Note that as in the case of statement (A), wherein r could be conceived as one satisfying the partial description p and in addition possibly possessing all CPs of the infinite sequence C_1, C_2, C_3, ... *ad inf.* cumulatively, in the case of statement (B) analogously, r can be conceived as one satisfying the partial description p and in addition possibly possessing all CPs of any infinite branch of the infinite tree-diagram cumulatively.

We now prove statement (B). For this, it is sufficient to prove that:

(a) There exists a mutually repellent pair of CPs, either CP of which can possibly be considered as giving the 1st additional bit of information about r, and

(b) If any finite sequence of n CPs for any natural number n is such that:

(i) The 1st CP of the sequence can possibly be considered as giving the 1st additional bit of information about r, the 2nd CP of the sequence can possibly be considered as giving the 2nd additional bit of information about r ... the $n-1^{th}$ CP of the sequence can possibly be considered as giving the $n-1^{th}$ additional bit of information about r and the last and n^{th} CP of the sequence can possibly be considered as giving the nth additional bit of information about r, and

(ii) All n CPs of the sequence in conjunction with p yet leave r partially described;

It necessarily follows that there exists a mutually repellent pair of CPs, either CP of which can possibly be considered as giving the $n+1^{th}$ additional bit of information about r.

Proof of (a): The assumption that no mutually repellent pair of CPs as defined in (a) exists, implies that any mutually repellent pair of CPs is such that one of its CPs is a CP of r and the other is not, which implies that r is already completely described, which contradicts the assumption that r is only partially described by p.

Proof of (b): Analogous to the above proof, but here assumptions (i) and (ii) require that r be considered as partially described by all n CPs of the finite sequence of n CPs under consideration in conjunction with p as compared to only p as in (a).

With this we conclude this article and follow it up with a key proposition.

7. Proposition: Any definable set S of real numbers that has an unspecifiable real number as element, has the power of the continuum.

Proof: Consider statement (B). If the partial description p in this statement is such that irrespective of which CP or conjunction of any finite number of CPs is regarded as in fact giving the 1st additional bit of information about r, there exists another CP which can possibly be considered as giving yet more information about r, conditions (a) and (b) of (6) can be proved as already demonstrated even without assumption (ii) of (b) and statement (B) can be replaced by the following statement:

'If r denotes a particular real number partially described by means of some partial description p of the type defined in the above paragraph, there exists a mutually repellent pair of CPs, either CP of which can possibly be considered as giving the 1st additional bit of information about r, and if $<C_0, C_1>$ denotes any particular such mutually repellent pair of CPs, either CP of this pair can in fact be considered the 1st additional bit of information about r, then if C_0 is in fact considered the 1st additional bit of information about r (information in addition to that given by p), there exists a 2nd pair of mutually repellent CPs, either CP of which can possibly be considered as giving the 2nd additional bit of information about r and if $<C_{00}, C_{01}>$ denotes any particular such 2nd mutually repellent pair of CPs, either CP of this pair can in fact be considered the 2nd additional bit of information about r, the 1st additional bit of information about r being C_0; similarly if C_1 is in fact considered the 1st additional bit of information about r (information in addition to that given by p), there exists a 2nd pair of mutually repellent CPs, either CP of which can possibly be considered as giving the 2nd additional bit of information about r and if $<C_{10}, C_{11}>$ denotes any particular such 2nd mutually repellent pair of CPs, either CP of this pair can in fact be considered the 2nd additional bit of information about r, the 1st additional bit of information about r being C_1; ... *ad inf.* ... (C).

In particular, if p denotes 'is an unspecifiable element of S', where S is any well-defined set of real numbers, p is of the type in statement (C) above and the infinite sequences of CPs in statement (C) for this p can be depicted by means of the infinite tree diagram and r can be conceived as one satisfying the partial description 'is an unspecifiable element of S' and in addition possibly possessing all CPs of any infinite branch of the infinite tree diagram, taken cumulatively.

If we now regard the infinite tree-diagram as depicting a collection C of all infinite branches, the result of the previous paragraph permits us to say that to each element/infinite branch of C, it is possible to correspond at least one unspecifiable element of S which possesses all the CPs of that infinite branch cumulatively and moreover such a functional correspondence C→S is one-one since any two distinct infinite branches are such that whereas one infinite branch has one of the CPs of some mutually repellent pair of CPs as its nth CP for some particular natural number n, the other infinite branch has the other CP of the mutually repellent pair as its nth CP, so it is impossible for them to correspond to the same unspecifiable element of S.

It follows that since C has the power of the continuum (it can be put in one-one onto correspondence with the set of all denumerable digit combinations of the numbers 0 and 1, which has the power of the continuum) and there exists a one-one functional correspondence C→S, some subset of S has the power of the continuum, whence by the corollary to (4), S has the power of the continuum.

Comment: Consider any arbitrary branch of the infinite tree diagram.

Say it is: $C_0 \rightarrow C_{00} \rightarrow C_{000} \rightarrow \ldots$ *ad inf.*

Note that although we <u>correspond</u> this to 0000 ... *ad inf.* in our proof, the branch does <u>not</u> depict the real number 0.000 ... *ad inf.* In fact if it did it would be a contradiction, since 0.000 ... *ad inf.* is the specifiable 'zero', which is clearly not an unspecifiable.

8. <u>Proposition (CONTINUUM HYPOTHESIS)</u>: There exists no definable set with cardinal number between that of a denumerable set and a set having the power of the continuum.

<u>Proof</u>: It is sufficient to prove CH for definable sets of real numbers alone, since its validity for such sets implies that it is valid for definable sets in general, since the contrary assumption that CH is valid for definable sets of real numbers but not valid for definable sets in general, implies that there exists a definable set, say S, that has cardinal number between that of a denumerable set and a set having the power of the continuum, which implies that S can be mapped by some mapping f into the set of all real numbers, which implies that f(S) is a definable set of real numbers having cardinal number between that of a denumerable set and a set having the power of the continuum, which contradicts the assumption that CH is valid for definable sets of real numbers.

By proposition (2), any infinite definable set which consists exclusively of specifiable real numbers is denumerable and since proposition (7) proves that any definable set of real numbers that has an unspecifiable real number as element has the power of the continuum, CH is proved.

This completes Part I.

Part II: The Paradoxes

9. <u>Introduction</u>: Although Part I was essentially treated rigorously, it was expounded within an intuitive framework. This needs some justification knowing as we do that the whole structure of intuitive mathematics has been considered inconsistent in recent years.

In particular, the proof of CH necessitates use of the concepts 'specifiable' and 'unspecifiable' and the question arises whether the free use of these terms is justified. We consider some definable set S and readily use the expression 'unspecifiable element of S' in regard to it. Are we justified in doing this? The following argument apparently seems to suggest that the answer to this question is a 'no'!

Assuming that our intuitive conception of a 'specifiable real number' is sound, it is possible to conceive an enumeration of all the specifiable real numbers. Now consider for this enumeration, the real number 'd' obtained by the diagonal process as in the proof exhibiting the set of all real numbers to be non-enumerable. Question: Is d a specifiable or an unspecifiable? Answer: By definition, d cannot be a specifiable, but nor can it be said to be an unspecifiable, since it has been uniquely expressed! Thus it appears that a fundamental concept of specifiables and unspecifiables is put in doubt: These were so defined that any real that is not a specifiable is an unspecifiable and vice-versa, so how is it possible for some real to be neither? Unless such questions are satisfactorily answered, the free use of the terms 'specifiable' and 'unspecifiable' in any expression would be questionable and the results of Part I would not be convincing, so let us see what we come up with.

10. <u>Berry's Paradox</u>[8]: Before the paradoxes, the question of the 'existence' of sets had never been posed. Cantor defined a set to be 'a collection of definite, distinguishable objects of our perception which can be conceived as a whole'. More specifically, Cantor and his early followers accepted the 'common sense' notion that if we can describe a property of entities, we can also speak of the set of all entities possessing that property. The paradoxes had the singular merit of proving this naïve conception of sets to be unacceptable – if only because certain properties led to paradoxical sets.

The paradoxes of set theory are of two different kinds, the one called 'logical' paradoxes, the other 'semantic' paradoxes. The reasons for the names 'logical' and 'semantic' will become clear to us when we have seen a few examples of these paradoxes;

---

[8] Charles C. Pinter, *Set Theory* (Bucknell University: Addison-Wesley Publishing Co., Inc., 1971) Chapter 0 Historical Introduction, 2 The paradoxes, Page 4

essentially, the 'logical' paradoxes arise from faulty 'logic' whereas the 'semantic' paradoxes arise from the faulty use of language.

We will devote the remainder of this section to the presentation of 'Berry's Paradox', one of the most celebrated of the semantic paradoxes, which involves only elementary concepts of set theory.

For the sake of argument, let us admit that all the words of the English language are listed in some standard dictionary. Let T be 'the set of all natural numbers that can be described in fewer that twenty words of the English language'. Since there are only a finite number of English words, there are only finitely many combinations of fewer than twenty such words, so T is a finite set. Quite obviously then, there are natural numbers which are greater than all the elements of T, hence there is a 'least natural number which cannot be described in fewer than twenty words of the English language'. By definition, this number is not in T; yet we have described it in sixteen words, hence it is in T!

When we reach a contradiction like this, we are forced to admit that one of our assumptions is false. Since the above argument is unimpeachable if 'T exists' is assumed, this assumption cannot be made! But how can this happen? If it is assumed that certain natural numbers <u>can</u> be described in fewer than twenty words of the English language and the remaining <u>cannot</u> be so described, we can produce a finite set of natural numbers, say F, by actually listing precisely those natural numbers that can be described in fewer than twenty words of the English language, so that T can be 'logically conceived' as the set F!

The situation compels us to admit that although T cannot be considered to exist in the conventional sense, it can nevertheless be logically conceived! This apparently contradictory aspect of T arises only because of the assumption that T can be <u>described</u> in terms of the expression expressing it (the expression 'the set of all natural numbers that can be described in fewer than twenty words of the English language' by which it is logically conceived) which is implied by the assumption 'T exists'. If such an assumption is not made, no paradox seems to result, since then the expression 'least number which cannot be described in fewer than twenty words of the English language' in turn is not required to be regarded a legitimate description of any natural number!

Generally speaking, any set-theoretic paradox, that is, paradox associated with any arbitrary paradoxical 'set' S, in fact ensues because the assumption 'S exists' is made, which conventionally is considered equivalent to 'there exists a set which can be <u>described</u> in terms of the expression S', which henceforth will be referred to as the 'strong assumption'. In certain cases however, the assumption 'there exists a set which can be <u>logically conceived</u> in terms of the expression S', which is relatively 'weaker' than the strong assumption (in the sense that whereas it is implied by the strong assumption, the converse is not the case) and which will henceforth be referred to as the 'weak assumption' is sufficient to deduce the paradox.

Paradoxes which cannot be deduced from the weak assumption alone but only from the strong assumption, like Berry's paradox, together with those which can be deduced from the weak assumption alone, fall into two mutually exclusive and exhaustive classes of paradoxes, the former being called the 'semantic' paradoxes and the latter 'logical' paradoxes, on account, in a manner of speaking, of the former stemming from the 'faulty use of language' and the latter 'faulty logic'. The semantic paradoxes can be logically conceived but not described in terms of the expressions by which they are conceived and hence may be regarded relatively 'weaker' paradoxes, requiring as they do the strong assumption for their deduction. Comparatively, the logical paradoxes, cannot even be logically conceived and hence may be regarded relatively 'stronger' paradoxes.

A crucial aspect of Berry's set T, one that ensures that it can be logically conceived as the set F, is that its defining property merely segregates certain natural numbers from the 'parent set' of all natural numbers which is already assumed to exist. Intuitively, it is clear that any defining property that merely segregates certain elements from others of some parent set which can be assumed or established to exist, produces a set which is at least logically conceivable if not also describable in terms of the expression by which it is conceived.

It follows that if a paradoxical set S has a parent set P, that is, there exists a legitimate set P which can be considered the parent set of S, then S is a semantic paradoxical set since any set that has a parent set can at least be logically conceived. Conversely, a logical paradoxical set can never have a parent set, since if it did, it would also be a semantic paradoxical set, which is impossible, the two being mutually exclusive.

We conclude this article with a comment as to why semantic paradoxical sets are in fact paradoxical. This happens if and only if some defining property has as basis for segregation some criterion that is variant (changing) accordingly as whether or not the set is assumed to be describable in terms of the expression by which it is logically conceived. For example, the defining property of the set of all rational numbers, being invariant in this sense, can never be paradoxical and on the other hand, the defining property of Berry's paradoxical set T has as basis for segregation a variant criterion: if T is <u>not</u> assumed to be describable in terms of the expression by which it is logically conceived, it is identical to F which has no natural number element which can be described by means of the sixteen-word contradictory expression 'least natural number which cannot be described in fewer than twenty words of the English language' and on the other hand if T <u>is</u> assumed to be describable in terms of the expression by which it is logically conceived, it necessarily has to have as element the natural number which can be logically conceived by the sixteen-word contradictory expression.

11. <u>Richard's Paradox</u>: We now take up for discussion the paradoxical set we are most interested in from the stand point of Part I of the paper: Richard's semantic paradoxical set R, whose treatment is somewhat analogous to that of Berry's paradoxical set T.

Once again we consider the English language, with its pre-assigned alphabet, dictionary and grammar. By an 'expression' of the English language, we may understand simply any finite sequence of words of the English language.

Let R be the set of all specifiable real numbers, that is, real numbers that can be finitely described by means of an expression of the English language. Since the expressions of the English language are enumerable, R is an enumerable set. Now consider for some enumeration of R, the real number 'd' obtained by the diagonal process as in the proof exhibiting the set of all real numbers to be non-enumerable. By definition, d is not in R; yet we have defined it finitely, hence it <u>is</u> in R! Once again, a glaring contradiction!

Since the above argument would be unimpeachable if we admit the existence of R, we are compelled to say that a set such as R simply cannot be said to exist. But how can this happen? If it is assumed that certain real numbers <u>can</u> be described in a finite number of words of the English language and the remaining <u>cannot</u> be so described, R <u>can</u> be logically conceived to be some set, say I, consisting precisely of those real numbers that <u>can</u> be described in a finite number of words of the English language!

This apparent contradiction that on the one hand a set such as R cannot be said to exist but on the other hand R can be logically conceived as the set I, forces us to the startling conclusion that whereas a set such as R cannot be said to exist, it can be logically conceived! As mentioned earlier, our point of departure from the earlier held view is that whereas the strong assumption 'r can be described in terms of the expression by which it is logically conceived' is yet considered equivalent to the assumption 'r exists', this is not so for the weak assumption 'r can be logically conceived' so that it is not contradictory to maintain that although 'r exists' cannot be said, 'r can be logically conceived' can be said!

Note that unlike the situation in Berry's paradox wherein the set F could actually be exhibited by listing its elements, the set I by comparison, being infinite, cannot be so exhibited.

We are now in a position to answer the question posed in the introduction: Is d a specifiable or an unspecifiable? Now we can emphatically say that it is an unspecifiable! This is so since although d can be logically conceived in terms of its expression which inextricably involves the logically conceivable but undefinable Richard's paradoxical set R, regarding this expression as a description of d would imply that d is a specifiable real number, which is impossible since d's 'description' is self-contradictory.

Our main task now seems to be over. One aim of incorporating Part II was to justify the intuitive approach in Part I and in particular answer the question posed in the above paragraph, which we seem to have done. We have also gained a sufficient insight as to when the semantic paradoxes occur and how to deal with them in an intuitive mathematical system and DPs of subsets of real numbers in which we were primarily interested in Part I yield at most only semantic paradoxical sets (if paradoxical at all) as already seen by virtue of the assumption that the parent set of all real numbers exists. For the sake of completeness however, it will be expedient now to dwell to some extent on the logical paradoxes. First we consider Russell's paradox.

12. <u>Russell's Paradox</u>: This is the simplest of the logical paradoxes. It can be described as follows:

Let A denote the 'set of all sets that are not elements of themselves'. Is A an element of itself? If A <u>is</u> an element of A, then by the very definition of A, A is <u>not</u> an element of A. If A is <u>not</u> an element of A, then again, because of the way A is defined, A <u>is</u> an element of A.

Thus we have proven that A is an element of A if and only if A is not an element of A – a contradiction of the most fundamental sort.

Here, unlike semantic paradoxical sets which could at least be logically conceived in terms of their expressions, no set can even be logically conceived in terms of A – the above argument simply precludes any such conception if it be assumed as we do that a set can be logically conceived in terms of A if and only if A is either an element of itself or not an element of itself. The set envisaged by A is simply an unrealizable collection that does not exist and nothing more can be said.

We now take up for discussion a logical paradox of fundamental importance: Cantor's paradox.

13. Cantor's Paradox: This paradox, concerning as it does the notion of the all-encompassing 'set of all sets', say S, is crucial and has a special significance in the theory of the logical paradoxes.

The paradox is that since every subset of S is also an element of S, on the one hand the power set of S, P(S), is a subset of S and the cardinal number of P(S) is less than or equal to the cardinal number of S but on the other hand, according to Cantor's theorem, the cardinal number of the power set of any arbitrary set is greater than the cardinal number of the set.

The situation here is analogous to that in Russell's paradox in the sense that the above argument is unimpeachable if it is even admitted that S can be logically conceived, let alone described in terms of its expression 'set of all sets', rendering S to be a logical paradoxical set.

The fact that S is in fact a logical paradoxical set can be established quite simply since the contrary assumption that it is a logically conceivable set implies that it is the parent set of Russell's paradoxical set A, which is impossible since A having been established to be a logical paradoxical set, cannot have any logically conceivable set as parent set.

Now it can be appreciated as to why it was earlier stated that the notion of S was crucial and had a special significance in the theory of the logical paradoxical sets. Notice that if S can be logically conceived, it can be considered to be the parent set of any logical paradoxical set, say L, however L, by definition being a logical paradoxical set, can never have any logically conceivable set as parent set, which implies that if there exists a single logical paradoxical set, S is not logically conceivable and conversely, if S is logically conceivable, no logical paradoxical set can exist!

With this we conclude our treatment of the logical paradoxes and proceed to our final article on the scope of Part I.

14. <u>The scope of Part I</u>: The scope of the Continuum Hypothesis result of Part I extends to include all sets which can intuitively be considered 'definable'. In particular, paradoxical sets of real numbers (which incidentally are of the semantic variety by virtue of their having the set of all real numbers as parent set) are also included in the scope. For example, the CH result of Part I is applicable to the 'set' of all specifiable real numbers (which is nothing but Richard's paradoxical set R) in the sense that the set logically conceived by R is denumerable, it consisting only of specifiable real numbers. Similarly, the 'set' of all unspecifiable real numbers, has the power of the continuum, it having an unspecifiable real number as element. In general, the concept of cardinal number of a paradoxical set P of real numbers is meaningful if it is interpreted to be the cardinal number of the set logically conceived by the expression P.

Notice however that although the novel idea that the above-mentioned semantic paradoxical sets can be logically conceived but cannot be described in terms of their respective expressions is employed to conceptualise such sets, the segregation of entities by the DPs of these sets is not based on any such novel idea. The DP of the paradoxical set of all specifiable real numbers for example, merely segregates the specifiable real numbers from the remaining ones and the above-mentioned novel idea is not required to achieve this segregation since no novel idea is required to distinguish a specifiable real number from an unspecifiable one.

Consider now the set $\{x \mid x = d$, where d is the diagonal element expressed in Richard's paradoxical set R$\}$. This is clearly the empty set ϕ, since no real number can be described in terms used to express d. On the other hand, the 'set' $\{x \mid x$ is the real number logically conceived (but not described) in terms of the expression used to express d$\}$ is not empty — in fact it is a singleton set, but unlike the paradoxical set of all specifiable real numbers or all unspecifiable real numbers or the empty set $\{x \mid x = d\}$ in which the segregation of entities by the sets' respective DPs is not based on the above-mentioned novel idea, this sets' DP is based on this novel idea, since it is meaningful if and only if it is assumed that d can be logically conceived but not described in terms of the expression used to express it!

It is clear that prior to the recognition of the existence of the novel idea under discussion, the intuitively allowable DPs of sets in intuitive set theory obviously did not include DPs based on this novel idea and nor was it considered necessary to do so since the range of intuitively allowable DPs not based on this idea was considered precisely that desired for the purposes of intuitive set theory. The results of this paper too are valid for only such DPs: The CH result of Part I is valid for all definable sets, even the paradoxical ones, but a 'set' such as $\{x \mid x$ is the real number logically conceived (but not described) in terms of the expression used to express d} whose DP <u>is</u> based on the novel idea is neither considered a legitimate definable set nor included in the scope of the CH result; in fact considering such a set as a legitimate singleton definable set yields a contradiction since the unspecifiable real number which is its sole element would then have to be considered definable in terms of its DP, which is impossible.

We conclude with the remark that unless otherwise stated, CPs and DPs in this paper will be understood to include all and only those which do <u>not</u> employ the novel idea as basis for segregation.

Part III: Implications for Continuum Hypothesis on Account of Axiom of Choice

The proof of the Continuum Hypothesis (CH) in Part I of this article was confined to definable sets within an intuitive framework. Differences between the intuitive and axiomatic approach primarily arise because of the intuitively compelling but highly controversial Axiom of Choice (AC). This article will analyse the consequences, especially in regard to CH, that occur when AC is included in the set of axioms of axiomatic set theory.

Consider that formulation of AC that assures the existence of a set 's' of 'representatives' consisting of any one 'representative' element from each of the members of a family 'f' of sets. A suitable selection of f then allows s to be any imaginable collection whatsoever.

Now, 'set' in axiomatic set theory being a primitive notion with axioms alone defining which 'structures' can be considered sets, and with AC implying the existence of a set s which can be any imaginable collection whatsoever, the categories of set include any structure assured to exist by the axioms in conjunction with the set s assured to exist by AC.

It can readily be seen from this, that the permissible categories of 'set' include the primitive notion 's' of set, resulting in a 'circular' non-explicit categorisation of sets, with the consequence that any property of sets dependant on explicit categorisation remains undecidable, and in particular CH remains undecidable.

This undecidablility of CH when AC is included in the axioms in axiomatic set theory is because of the non-constructive nature of AC, which is basically only an existential statement.

15

The Search for Happiness

We find ourselves in a bewildering world and need calming influences as balm for our souls.

Neither science nor religion is adequate and fundamental philosophical questions had hitherto remained unanswered.

It is values, courage and compassion, tempered with practicality, that is most enduring in this ultracompetitive age.

Sometimes, paradoxically, the more we try to be 'happy', the less happy we become! Why? Because focusing on 'how to be happy' presumes we are unhappy and the mind goes around in circles and cannot shake off its despondency.

We must remember that our minds' function is based on natural laws over which we have no control and it seems that the mind will go on and on trying to resolve unresolvable issues or moods it perceives detrimental to itself.

The mind can, however, by conscious effort, be diverted. Any interest or passion effectively diverts minds and induces happiness. In particular the metaphysical concept of Determinism is widely acknowledged to induce serenity. It is felt 'what will be, will be'.

16

The Song of Love

In love, man finds his greatest fulfilment. Nothing so enthuses, gives meaning to it all and uplifts spirits to exuberance.

Be that as it may, why the compelling need to 'understand' love? To harmonize it with desire? But it is doubtful if understanding alone would do this.

Although there is a 'mechanism' governing love, it is beyond science. It is impossible to capture the spirit of love analytically. A poem or song or a work of art fares better here. It is as if to one who has experienced love, no explanation is required and to one who hasn't, no explanation is possible. Maybe this is just as well, maybe love is magical <u>because</u> it cannot be explained!

It is not as if decipherable patterns of love do not exist. They exist, but invariably have unexpected exceptions. Intuition alone navigates the waters of love as best it can.

As is well known, there is also a dark side to love. Love can make or break the strongest ones, but as the saying goes 'it is better to have loved and lost than never to have loved at all'.

Love does not necessarily come to the virtuous, but this should not deter the pursuit of virtuosity, which can be a great source of fulfilment in its own right and which, unlike love, seemingly depends on our will alone.

17

God

Unlike us who think we are free but are in fact not,
God is totally free without doubt.
You see, He could have left it all a void,
But this He decided to avoid.

God has his reasons and for all there is an explanation,
But not necessarily within the scope of our comprehension.
Think of God as Nature: Omnipresent and Omnipotent;
This view is most consistent.

God has it all determined but one should act as if free,
Otherwise I am sorry you would be barking up the wrong tree.
Seek answers by identifying your conscience with God,
Which although not easy is neither too hard.

The pursuit of happiness is the meaning of it all you would agree,
But achieving this is not that easy.
Only when finally you decide to make God happy,
It is you in fact that ends up happy.

Printed in the United States
By Bookmasters